CELEBRITY SECRETS

EXTREME SPORTS STARS

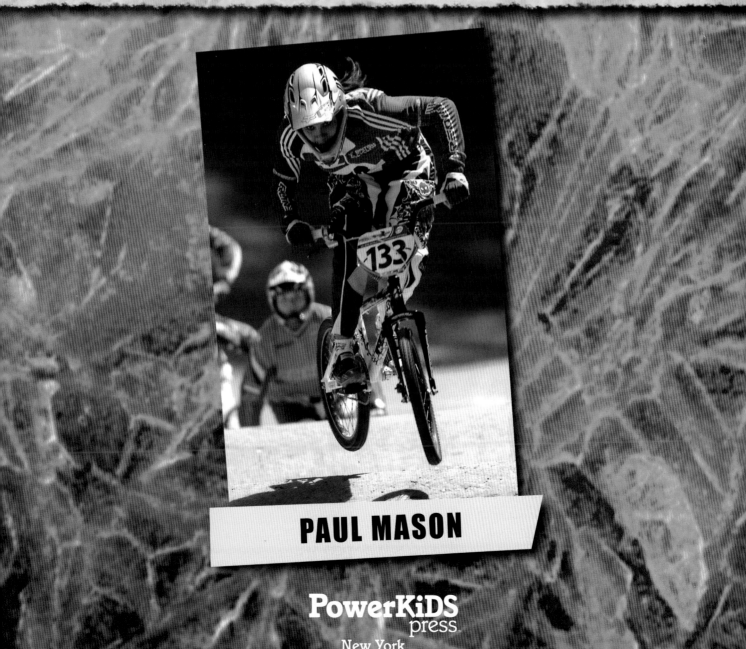

PAUL MASON

PowerKiDS
press
New York

Published in 2012 by The Rosen Publishing Group, Inc.
29 East 21st Street, New York, NY 10010

First Edition

Editor: Julia Adams
Designer: Stephen Prosser
Picture Researcher: Julia Adams
Indexer and Proofreader: Rebecca Clunes

Picture Acknowledgments: The author and publisher would like to thank the following for allowing their pictures to be reproduced in this publication:
Cover and p21: Sipa Press/Rex Features; p1 and p13: Troy Wayrynen/ NewSport/Corbis; p2 and p8: PCN Photography/Alamy; p4: AFP/Getty Images; p5: Getty Images; p6: Mason Brownlow/Rex Features; p7: Photos 12/Alamy; p9: Getty Images; p10: Getty Images Sport; p11: Aurora Photos/Alamy; p12: Getty Images; ; p14: ASP/CI via Getty Images; p15: Shutterstock; p16: Time & Life Pictures/Getty Images; p17: Sports Illustrated/Getty Images; p18:Bo Bridges/Corbis; p20: Shutterstock; p19: Osports.cn/NewSport/Corbis; p22 (top): Getty Images Sport; p22 (centre): AP/Press Association Images; p22 (bottom): Buzz Pictures/Alamy; p23 (top): Sports Illustrated/Getty Images; p23 (centre): Shutterstock; p23 (bottom): Guillem Lopez/Alamy.

Library of Congress Cataloging-in-Publication Data

Mason, Paul, 1967–
 Extreme sports stars / by Paul Mason —1st ed.
      p. cm. — (Celebrity secrets)
 Includes index.
 ISBN 978-1-4488-7035-6 (library binding) — ISBN 978-1-4488-7080-6 (pbk.) — ISBN 978-1-4488-7081-3 (6-pack)
 1. Athletes—United States—Biography—Juvenile literature. 2. Extreme sports—Juvenile literature. I. Title.
 GV697.A1.M352 2012
 796.0922—dc23
                                        2011029064

Manufactured in Malaysia

CPSIA Compliance Information: Batch #WW2102PK: For Further Information contact Rosen Publishing, New York, New York at 1-800-237-9932

Contents

Anne-Caroline Chausson

FRENCH SUPER-CYCLIST

Anne-Caro with her 2008 Olympic gold medal for BMX.

Anne-Caroline Chausson has won a record 55 victories in the world's top-level bike races. No other rider has come close to this.

Stats!

Name: Anne-Caroline Chausson

Date of birth: October 8, 1977

Based: Dijon, France

Famous as: Multiple world champion mountain biker and Olympic BMX gold medalist.

First break: Anne-Caroline (or Anne-Caro) broke into downhill mountain biking in 1993. It was her first year on the circuit, but Anne-Caro won the junior downhill world championship. She went on to win again in 1994 and 1995 before moving to the senior championships in 1996.

Major achievements: Downhill mountain-biking: twelve-time world champion, including three junior titles and four-time winner of the World Cup. Dual slalom: four-time world champion, two-time winner of the World Cup; 4X: two-time world champion; BMX: three-time world champion; 2008 Olympic champion.

Secrets of her success: Anne-Caroline is such a great rider because she is able to relax even while riding the trickiest downhill routes. This saves energy and allows her to ride faster than anyone else on the last part of the course.

Life Story

Anne-Caroline Chausson was born in Dijon, France. She took to bike racing from a very young age. She won the under-10 years BMX world championship in 1987. In 1993 Anne-Caro gave up BMX and began to compete in downhill mountain biking instead.

She was only 15, but Anne-Caro was an immediate success. Her brilliant bike control and fearless late braking made her the fastest junior around and she won the junior world championship three times.

In 1996, when Anne-Caro started racing as a senior, her greatest rival was racer Missy Giove, from the United States. Although Giove was far more experienced, Anne-Caro won the world championship in her first year as a senior. She went on to win it another eight times.

Anne-Caro also took part in Dual and 4X contests. In these, riders race side-by-side down a course (2 riders in Dual, 4 in 4X). She won another four world championships in these events before retiring from racing in 2005.

In 2008 Anne-Caro came out of retirement and was chosen for the French Olympic BMX team. Three years after retiring from the sport, she won Olympic gold. It was the first time BMX racing had been in the Olympics, so Anne-Caro became the first-ever Olympic BMX champion.

Questions and Answers

Q Is there any surface Anne-Caroline can't ride fast on?

"Well, she smoked it in the snow. I started next to her and I watched her—she was amazing. She went straight for the snow and was just so fast—she's crazy. She definitely dominates this race!"

Anne-Caro's friend and fellow racer Sabrina Jonnier after the 2009 Megavalanche race

Q Can Anne-Caro's comeback to downhill racing succeed?

"I did a practice run with Anne-Caroline and I thought to myself, 'There is no way anyone is going to go faster than her'. [On my way] down the course I could hear her behind me! I pulled over and let her pass; I knew she was going to win today."

American racer Leigh Donovan after Anne-Caro had won the Monster Energy Garbanzo Downhill in 2010

5

Sébastien Foucan

FREERUNNER AND ACTOR

Sébastien stands in the area where his freerunning career began, the town of Lisses, near Paris, France.

One of Sébastien's first heroes was the martial arts expert and actor Bruce Lee.

Stats!

Name: Sébastien Foucan

Date of birth: May 24, 1974

Based: Paris, France

Famous as: One of the founders of freerunning; he is now a well-known actor.

First break: Sébastien first became famous when he appeared in a 2003 documentary called *Jump London*. Sébastien and two other freerunners were shown performing their amazing techniques among some of London's most famous buildings. The film was so successful that a sequel, *Jump Britain*, was made.

Major achievements:
2003: Appears in the documentary films *Jump London* and *Jump Britain*.
2005: Performs in the video for Madonna's single "Jump."
2006: Plays the villain Mollaka in the James Bond film *Casino Royale*. Involved in choreography and performance on Madonna's Confessions tour.
2007: Appears in the movie *The Tournament*, with Robert Carlyle. Works on the development of a freerunning-specific shoe.
2008: Publishes *Freerunning: Find Your Way*, his first book.

Secrets of his success: Sébastien would probably say that he has been successful because he always tries to improve. He always wants to find a better technique for freerunning and find ways to make old techniques better.

Life Story

Sébastien was born in a poor suburb of Paris. As kids, he and his friends used to run around, making up stories about how crocodiles lived in walkways and similar tales. To avoid the crocodiles and other hazards, they would have to climb walls, jump gaps, and climb along railings. All these skills would later become part of freerunning.

Questions and Answers

Q Did you train every day when you first got into parkour?

A *"Erm, no, no no, at the beginning, not every day. Not for me. It was just a play around sometimes, just maybe four or five times a week. Always after school."*

(Interviewed in 2004, quoted on www.parkourpedia.com)

Q Can you tell us what parkour and freerunning are about?

A *"No violence, no competition, no groups, no chiefs. The way of the parkour is to [keep moving], not to stay here. You can find the way by yourself naturally, you just need a guide to tell you to be careful, to not do this to impress people, just follow your instincts."*

(quoted on www.parkour.nl)

In 1987, Sébastien met a teenager named David Belle. David had begun to create what he called parkour, an activity that involved running through the town in the same way Sébastien and his friends had as kids. Sébastien, David, and several others who practiced together founded a group called Yamakasi. The members of Yamakasi developed most of the basic moves of parkour.

By 2001, Sébastien had begun to create a new style of parkour, which he called freerunning. It was more gymnastic and spectacular than parkour. Freerunning looked great on film and Sébastien was soon in demand to take part in advertisements. Then the 2003 documentaries *Jump London* and *Jump Britain* made him the world's most famous freerunner. Sébastien began to appear in movies and today he works as an actor, as well as teaching freerunning.

You'd run like this, too, if you had an angry James Bond chasing you!

Lewis Hamilton

SUPERSTAR RACER

Lewis has raced for the McLaren team since long before his first Formula 1 race.

Lewis isn't only good at driving fast, he's also a martial arts expert. In fact, he was a black belt at karate by the time he was 12 years old.

Stats!

Name: Lewis Carl Davidson Hamilton

Date of birth: January 7, 1985

Born: Stevenage, UK

Famous as: One of the most talented and aggressive drivers in the Formula 1 (F1) world championship.

First break: Lewis's career took a big step forward at an awards ceremony in 1995. There he met Ron Dennis, who ran the McLaren motorsports team at the time. Dennis remembers Lewis introducing himself, then saying that he was going to drive for McLaren one day. Today, Lewis drives for McLaren and has already won one F1 world championship for the team.

Major achievements:
2000: Ranked #1 in the world in karting.
2006: GP2 Champion.
2007: Grand Prix debut at age 22; becomes youngest driver ever to lead the world championship; wins four races and loses out on first place in the world championship by one point.
2008: Wins five races and becomes Formula 1 world champion.
2010: Wins three races and comes 4th in the world championship after the hardest-fought F1 season for years.

Secrets of his success: Lewis himself says that the secret of his success is a combination of talent, hard work, and love of the sport: "If I didn't love it, I'm sure I wouldn't be as good as I am today because I wouldn't have put half the effort in."

Life Story

Lewis Hamilton started racing go-karts at 6 years old. It wasn't long before the owner of the local track was joking that Lewis would one day be world champion. He soon came to the attention of the McLaren race team boss Ron Dennis, and was signed up for McLaren's Young Driver Support Programme. It was the start of his amazing success in motor racing.

Lewis Hamilton winning the Canadian Grand Prix in 2007.

In his first Formula 1 season in 2007, he finished in the top three in the first nine races, won four races, was on pole position (the best position at the start of the race) six times, and won 109 points. No other driver had ever beaten any of these records. The following year, 2008, Lewis did even better. He won the world championship.

The next year, 2009, was one of the toughest seasons of Lewis's career, but in 2010, things began to improve. Lewis managed to finish fourth in the championship. His McLaren car was more competitive and Lewis came close to winning the world championship again. He could not manage it, but with three wins and five second place finishes, it looked like Lewis was heading back to the top.

Questions and Answers

Q What's it like driving a Formula 1 car?

A *"You wouldn't believe what it's like in the car, the forces that are on you. I finish every race with a black line down my side where I've been pushed against the seat. But the race is the most exciting part, the first corner, the first pit stop."*

Lewis Hamilton, Observer Sport Monthly, *June 2007.*

Q What's it like to be the first black Formula 1 driver?

A *"Being the first black man [to race in Formula 1] doesn't mean much to me personally, but to the sport it probably means quite a lot."*

Lewis Hamilton, Daily Telegraph

Lynn Hill

INSPIRATIONAL RECORD BREAKER

The hardest move on a climb like this one is known as the crux. Very few crux moves have ever defeated Lynn Hill.

In 1988, Lynn married climber Russ Raffa. The ceremony took place while they were dangling from a cliff on ropes, dressed in their wedding outfits.

Stats!

Name: Lynn Hill

Date of birth: 1961

Based: Moab, Utah

Famous as: Record-setting female rock climber who has climbed more extreme rock faces than anyone, male or female.

First break: Lynn first became famous among rock climbers in 1979 when she climbed a route called Ophir Broke in Colorado. Ophir Broke was graded 5.12+/5.13, which meant it was an extremely difficult climb. Lynn was the first woman anywhere in the world to finish a climb of this difficulty.

Major achievements: Lynn started out setting records for female climbers, but then went on to do things no climber, male or female, had ever done before.
1986–1992: Over 30 victories in international climbing contests.
1991: First woman to finish a climb graded 5.14, Masse Critique, in France.
1993: First ever to climb The Nose in California without climbing aids.
1994: First person to climb The Nose in 24 hours (the route usually takes even the most skilled climbers four or more days).

Secrets of her success: Lynn's success as a climber is partly due to her natural gifts. She is strong and light and has extremely good coordination and balance. She is also brave, confident, and not afraid of taking risks during a climb.

Life Story

Born in Michigan, Lynn Hill actually grew up in southern California. When she was 14 years old, Lynn's older sister and her sister's boyfriend took her on a climbing and camping trip for the first time. Lynn was quickly hooked on climbing, and it wasn't long before she was spending her free time rock climbing.

Questions and Answers

Q What was the climbing scene like when you started?

A *"We were oddballs. That's the way climbing was. It was so unknown. Now it's everywhere and people have an image of it in their minds."*

Lynn Hill, Observer Sport, *May 2002*

Q What was it like climbing the hardest section of The Nose?

A *"Knowing that I could easily fall off at any moment, I had faith that I could make it only if I kept moving. So instead of stopping in the middle of the roof to clip my rope into a key piece of protection, I risked it and kept climbing."*

Climbing Free *by Lynn Hill*

Lynn Hill climbs the tricky route Esplendido in the Vinales valley, Cuba.

Lynn's most famous climbs have been in Yosemite Valley, California. Yosemite is a deep valley hemmed in by giant rock faces up to 3,280 feet (1 km) high. One of the most famous routes is The Nose, where Lynn has set more than one record. Her most amazing feat was to climb The Nose in less than 24 hours. Eleven years passed before anyone finished the route in a faster time.

Today, Lynn is a climbing legend. After a 2004 contest, top Slovenian climber Martina Čufar said it had been "a big honor to climb with her. She's simply amazing." Lynn won that contest. She is still a fierce competitor and a great climber, despite her age. She has organized several climbing camps and continues to inspire young women to get into the sport.

Shanaze Reade

FAST-STARTING BMX BLASTER

Shanaze Reade is one of the most feared competitors in BMX racing.

In 2006, Shanaze became the British #1 in the Over-19 BMX division, despite being only 17 years old. Even more surprising, she was also #1 in the men's division!

Stats!

Name: Shanaze Danielle Reade

Date of birth: September 23, 1988

Based: Manchester, UK

Famous as: One of the world's most powerful BMX and track cyclists.

First break: One of Shanaze's closest advisors when she started racing was Jamie Staff, a former BMX racer who went on to become a world and Olympic champion at track cycling. Like Staff, Shanaze went to race in the United States as a way of building her experience. She won her first pro race, the U.S. Winter National Championships, there in 2006.

Major achievements:
2006: Junior BMX world champion.
2007: Gold medalist (with Victoria Pendleton) in the Women's Team Sprint at the World Track Championships, in a world-record time.
2007: BMX world champion.
2008: Gold medalist (again with Victoria Pendleton) in the Women's Team Sprint at the World Track Championships, in another world-record time.
2008: BMX world champion.
2010: BMX world champion.

Secrets of her success: Shanaze is known as one of the most powerful riders on the BMX circuit. Her leg strength allows her to make fast starts and her overall strength makes jumps and fast turns easier to handle.

Life Story

Jordy Smith was born and grew up in Durban, South Africa. The city is a surfing hotspot, although with beach names like Shark Alley, you need to be brave to paddle out on a board! Jordy's local spot, New Pier, is protected from sharks by nets. That and the powerful waves have always made New Pier a popular place to surf. Because of the crowds, surfers compete for waves. When they get one, they have to make the most of it!

Questions and Answers

Q What's your favorite place in the world to go surfing?

A *"My favorite spot has to be my home break, New Pier [in Durban]. It's where I grew up surfing and where I get to surf with all my friends. If I had to choose another favorite spot it would have to be J-Bay [South Africa]."*

Jordy Smith, www.worldprosurfers.com, 2010

Q Who has been the biggest influence on you?

A *"If you ask me to name the people in the world who've influenced me most, it's always going to be my dad first. He's been a massive influence on my life. My dad is my manager, my coach, and my mentor."*

Jordy Smith, www.worldprosurfers.com, 2010

The conditions at New Pier turned Jordy into a competition machine. As a boy, he won ten South African national surfing titles. Jordy became known for doing aerial moves, getting such speed from the wave that he could use the wave as a ramp and launch himself above it. In 2007, Jordy won the World Qualifying Series (WQS), earning himself a place on the Dream Tour, surfing's top competition.

Jordy had a tough year in 2008. He struggled on the Dream Tour and just managed to keep his place for the next year. But in 2009 he surfed brilliantly and came close to winning the world championship. In the end, ten-time world champion Kelly Slater won, with Jordy coming in second. Jordy seems likely to go one better and become world champion before too long.

Jordy midway through one of his famed radical aerials.

Ann Trason

LEGENDARY ULTRARUNNING HERO

Ann Trason warms up after another punishing ultrarunning event.

During the 1990s, Ann set at least 12 course records that have still not been beaten today. But when told she was considered the greatest female ultrarunner ever, she replied: "Oh, I wouldn't say that... I don't believe in titles."

Stats!

Name: Ann Trason

Date of birth: August 30, 1960

Based: Kensington, California

Famous as: Legendary, record-setting ultrarunner

First break: Ann broke into the world of ultrarunning in her very first race. She says, "I wanted to run a marathon and saw an ad for a 50-mile (80 km) race. It seemed like it would take a little longer but it [needed] the same [approach], so I did it." She not only finished the American River 50 Mile Endurance Run, but also won.

Major achievements: In total, Ann Trason set over 20 world and course records during her endurance-running career. Highlights include:
1994: Course records in Western States 100 and Leadville Trail 100.
1995: World record in the World 100K Championship.
1996: Twelve days after winning the 56-mile (89 km) Comrades Marathon in South Africa, wins Western States 100 in the United States.
1997: Repeats Comrades Marathon/ Western States 100 double.

Secrets of her success: Ann once said that to succeed, you have to have the "right attitude." This means finding the positive things about any situation. For example, if it's raining in the winter, it means it's probably warmer than it could have been with no clouds overhead.

Life Story

Ann Trason was a good runner in school. She mostly ran on the track, because few women took part in trail-running events. Finding track running dull, she became interested in triathlons. She injured her arm when a car hit her bike while she was out training. Ann started to concentrate on running long distances and found she was extremely good at it.

In 1998, Ann had one of the most amazing years ever seen in ultrarunning. In a period of five months, she won five 100-mile (161 km) races: in June, the Western States 100; in July, the Vermont 100 Mile Endurance Run (in 17 hours and 11 minutes); in August, the Leadville Trail 100; September and October, the Wasatch Front 100 and Arkansas Traveller 100.

Ann Trason running in the Western States 100, which she has won 14 times.

Ann's most famous achievements have been in the Western States 100. Competitors race through the mountains of California. They start at 5 a.m. and continue through the day, into the night, and into the next day. Ann has won the Western States 100 14 times and is still the overall course record holder in the women's 18–29, 30–39, and 40–49 age groups.

Today, Ann has stopped taking part in ultrarunning competitions, but can still be spotted pounding the trails of California just for fun.

Questions and Answers

Q Which part of your running career are you most proud of?

A "The consistency—that I could finish Western States as many times as I did, through the different things that happened."

Ann Trason, Runner's World, 2008

Q Who most inspires you?

A "It's more the courses that have inspired me. I love where I've been and that's inspired me to try harder."

Ann Trason, Runner's World, 2008

Danny Way

HIGH-JUMPING SKATEBOARD STAR

Danny Way has launched some of the biggest aerials in skateboarding.

Danny was the first and so far the only skater ever to win *Thrasher Magazine*'s Skater of the Year award twice.

Stats!

Name: Daniel Way

Date of birth: April 15, 1974

Based: San Diego, California

Famous as: Great-Wall-of-China-leaping skateboarding superstar

First break: Danny started on the skateboarding contest scene at a very young age. His first competition was when he was just 11 years old. Amazingly, he won, and it wasn't long before he became a sponsored rider.

Major achievements:
1991, 2004: *Thrasher Magazine* Skater of the Year
1997: Breaks world record for highest aerial, with a 12 feet (3.7 m) high kickflip
2002: Sets new world skateboard long-jump and height records, with a distance of 65 feet (20 m) and height of 18 feet (5.5 m)
2004, 2005, 2006: X-Games gold medals
2005: Jumps Great Wall of China
2009: Breaks skateboard world speed record. Wins first-ever X-Games Big Air Rail Jam

Secrets of his success: Danny constantly pushes himself to go one better than before. At the X-Games 11, after winning gold on the mega ramp, he pulled off his sock and said: "That's what we're operating on today!" Danny had fractured his ankle several weeks before.

Life Story

Danny Way had a tough start. His father died when he was a baby, and his mother struggled to raise him alone. But when Danny's mother remarried, his stepfather introduced him to skateboarding. Danny threw himself into the sport. In fact, he loved skating so much that later on, he had "SK8" tattooed on one of his fingers.

Danny found that his favorite style of skateboarding was on vert ramps (half pipes with vertical sides). He immediately started winning contests and turned pro in 1989, when he was just 15 years old. Within a couple of years he was so good that *Thrasher Magazine* named him their Skater of the Year.

Danny was soon trying to push the limits of aerial skateboarding further than ever before. He built bigger and bigger ramps, including the first mega ramp. Danny's amazing leaps appeared in a video for DC Shoes, a company Danny and his brother Damon had helped set up. The mega ramp blew other skaters away. No one else was doing huge aerials like these. Danny's most amazing jump was in 2005, when he jumped the Great Wall of China.

Questions and Answers

Q   How did you start skateboarding at such a young age?

A   *"My dad realized how excited I was about the skate park, so he started taking me to Del Mar when I was five years old. At Del Mar, you had to be six years old to skate. My dad lied for me so I could skate."*

Danny Way, Juice: Pools, Pipes and Punk Rock, *2005*

Q   What got you into doing aerials on skateboards?

A   *"We'd drive down the Interstate 5 by the skate park. And I'd be looking out the window and seeing guys launching airs. I was just simply attracted to the principle of launching airs on skateboards. Every time we drove by, I was like a kid in the candy store watching for the thirty seconds I could see it."*

Danny Way, Juice: Pools, Pipes and Punk Rock, *2005*

Danny jumps the Great Wall of China. It was the first time anyone had managed to leap it using a non-motorized vehicle.

Shaun White

SKATE AND SNOWBOARD SUPERSTAR

Shaun White's laid-back California attitude hides a very competitive nature.

In 2003, when he was 18 years old, Shaun became the first person ever to get medals at both the summer and winter X-Games in the same year.

Stats!

Name: Shaun Roger White

Date of birth: September 3, 1986

Based: Colorado

Famous as: Being so good at both snowboarding and skating that it's hard to decide which is his best sport.

First break: Shaun's first break came along when he was just nine years old. He was spotted skateboarding by the legendary rider Tony Hawk, who became Shaun's mentor and adviser. Hawk kept track of Shaun and helped him turn pro as a skateboarder when he was 17 years old.

Major achievements: Shaun is one of the world's best skateboarders, and his achievements in snowboarding beat just about any other rider's. He is a two-time Olympic halfpipe champion at snowboarding (2006 and 2010), has won six Dew Tour gold medals for snowboarding between 2008 and 2009, ten Winter X-Games gold medals between 2003 and 2010, and is the winner of one gold, two silver, and one bronze medal in vert contests at the Summer X-Games.

Secrets of his success: Shaun has amazing physical gifts, including incredible coordination and balance. He is also an extremely hard worker, spending hours every day working on his skills. "You have to keep pushing yourself," he says.

Life Story

Shaun was born with a heart problem. It meant that he had to have two operations on his heart before he was a year old. Despite this, even as a small boy Shaun loved sports, including soccer, surfing, and skiing. At six, he was so fast on skis that his mother said he had to ride a snowboard instead. She thought it would slow him down.

Within a year, Shaun was a good enough snowboarder to win contests. He became a sponsored rider for Burton, the biggest snowboard company around. At 13, Shaun turned pro, and three years later, in 2001, he won his first X-Games gold medal.

At the same time as all this was happening, Shaun was breaking through on the skateboarding scene. His skating was a little slower to get going than his snowboarding career. Shaun had to wait until he was 17 to sign a professional contract as a skateboarder.

Shaun has been the first to land some amazing moves, including the first back-to-back double cork on a snowboard and the first cab 7 melon grab in vert skateboarding. He has dominated snowboard pipe riding since 2003 and shows no sign of stopping.

Questions and Answers

Q   How did you manage at the half pipe when you were really small?

A   *"My dad would mainly carry me up [to the top of] the pipe. I wouldn't even unbuckle, I would just latch onto my dad and he'd bring me to the top. The best part was when I'd get to the bottom and my dad was still at the top, random people would get down low and I'd just jump on their back and head up to the top."*

Shaun White, Snowboarder Magazine, *2008*

Q   Which is more fun, snowboarding or skateboarding?

A   *"It depends. I have the most fun snowboarding when it's just me and my brother. I get so comfortable when I'm with people I like to ride with that I just start learning tricks. I think that's so much fun when snowboarding's like that."*

Shaun White, Snowboarder Magazine, *2008*

OTHER EXTREME SPORTS PEOPLE

Cara-Beth Burnside

Basic Information

Born and lives: Orange County, California

Birthday: July 23, 1968

Career, Likes, and Interests

Background: Cara-Beth proved that girls can hack it in extreme sports. She started skateboarding when she was 10, at a time when there were hardly any women skating. At 23 Cara-Beth started competing against men, because there were no women's contests. She took up snowboarding and within a few years was ranked # 2 in the world.

Career highs: Winner of over 16 major competitions, including two X-Games gold medals (one for skating, one for snowboarding); *Thrasher Magazine* female skateboarder of the year 2003; 2004 female vert skater of the year.

Other information: Incredibly versatile, good at skateboarding, snowboarding, and surfing.

Web site: http://espn.go.com/action/athlete/_/id/21/cara-beth-burnside

Yiannis Kouros

Career, Likes, and Interests

Background: Yiannis Kouros is the most successful ultrarunner ever. At one time, he held every men's ultrarunning record for distances between 100 miles (161 km) and 1000 miles (1,609 km), and for times between 12 hours and 6 days. He still holds the road-running records for 100 miles (161 km), and 1000 miles (1,609 km), plus various world records for distance covered in 12 hours, one day, two days and six days.

Career highs: Winner of the Spartathlon, one of the world's toughest ultra races, in 1983, 1984, 1986, and 1990. In the course of his career, Yiannis has broken over 100 world records.

Other information: As well as being a brilliant ultrarunner, Yiannis is a singer and musician, has recorded four albums, and is a poet.

Basic Information

Born: Tripolis, Greece. Now lives in Melbourne, Australia

Birthday: February 13, 1956

Web site: www.yianniskouros.com/

Layne Beachley

Career, Likes, and Interests

Background: Layne is the most successful female surfer of modern times. She became a pro surfer at 16 and between 1998 and 2003 was almost unbeatable in competition. In 2004, Layne became one of the very few women who have surfed in a men's contest. She is also one of a small number of women who have surfed successfully in waves of 20 feet (6 m) or more.

Career highs: Winner of the ASP World Surfing Championship 1998, 1999, 2000, 2001, 2002, 2003, and 2006.

Other information: Layne was the first woman ever to do tow-in surfing on the giant waves of Hawaii's outer reefs.

Basic Information

Born and lives: Sydney, Australia

Birthday: May 24, 1972

Web site: www.surfline.com/surfing-a-to-z/layne-beachley-biography-and-photos_755

Gretchen Bleiler

Career, Likes, and Interests

Background: Gretchen started snowboarding at the age of 11, after her family moved to Aspen, Colorado. She turned pro at 15 and in 2003, 2004, and 2005 won more snowboard half pipe contests than any other female snowboarder. As a small girl Gretchen had dreamed of going to the Olympics, and in 2006 she won a silver medal at the Winter Olympics. At the 2010 games, she fell on both of her final runs and finished 11th.

Career highs: Winter X-Games golds in the snowboard superpipe in 2003, 2005, 2008, and 2010.

Other information: As well as snowboarding, Gretchen rides a mountain bike and surfs. She is also an environmental activist.

Web site: www.gretchenbleiler.com/

Basic Information

Born: Toledo, Ohio. Now lives in Aspen, Colorado
Birthday: April 10, 1981

Kelly Slater

Career, Likes, and Interests

Background: Kelly Slater is without doubt the best competition surfer ever to paddle a surfboard. He has won an amazing 10 surfing world championships. The next most successful surfer is Mark Richards of Australia, who won five. Kelly is also something of a celebrity, having dated a string of famous women, including Pamela Anderson and Gisele Bundchen.

Career highs: Youngest surfer ever to win the world championship (at the age of 20). Oldest surfer ever to win the world championship (at 38). Five championships in a row 1994–1998. Winner of the Eddie Aikau Invitational big-wave contest in 2002.

Other information: Kelly has appeared in video games including *Kelly Slater's Pro Surfer* and *Tony Hawk's Pro Skater 3*.

Web site: www.kellyslater.com/

Basic Information

Born and lives: Cocoa Beach, Florida
Birthday: February 11, 1972

Tony Hawk

Career, Likes, and Interests

Background: Tony started skating when he was 9, after his brother gave him a blue fiberglass "banana board," so-called because most of them were yellow. By the time he was 14, Tony was good enough to turn pro. Two years later, he was acknowledged to be the best skater in the world. Tony invented many of vert skating's most radical tricks and also helped hundreds of other skaters with their careers. He is one of the founders of the Athletes for Hope charity.

Career highs: In 1999, he became the first skater to land a 900 (a jump featuring two-and-a-half aerial spins) in a competition or on video. Winner of nine X-Games gold medals on the vert ramp.

Other information: The *Tony Hawk's Pro Skater* computer game series is one of the most successful ever, with over 14 titles.

Web site: www.tonyhawk.com

Basic Information

Born and lives: San Diego, California
Birthday: May 12, 1968

Glossary

aerial (EHR-ee-ul) Of or in the air.

championship (CHAM-pee-un-ship) A contest held to determine the best, or the winner.

confidence (KON-fih-dents) A firm belief in oneself and one's abilities.

Formula 1 (FAWR-myuh-luh WUN) A kind of car used in racing. It has one seat and its wheels are on the outside of the car's body.

mentor (MEN-tor) A trusted guide or teacher.

skills (SKILZ) Abilities or things that help one do a job well.

techniques (tek-NEEKS) A way of doing something.

Index

Web Sites

Due to the changing nature of Internet links, PowerKids Press has developed an online list of Web sites related to the subject of this book. This site is updated regularly. Please use this link to access the list:
www.powerkidslinks.com/celeb/extreme/